Reassure the Phoenix

Reassure the Phoenix

Poems by

John David Muth

Kelsay Books

Copyright 2019 John David Muth. All rights reserved.
This material may not be reproduced in any form, published,
reprinted, recorded, performed, broadcast, rewritten
or redistributed without the explicit
permission of John David Muth.
All such actions are strictly prohibited by law.

Cover design: Shay Culligan

ISBN: 978-1-949229-95-0

Kelsay Books Inc.

kelsaybooks.com
502 S 1040 E, A119
American Fork, Utah 84003

To my father and the memory of my mother

Acknowledgments

Anti-Heroin Chic: "Laundry is Easy"

Better Than Starbucks!: "Asking Dad for Her Hand in Marriage."

Buck Off Magazine: "First Date Deceptions"

Misfit Magazine: "Hard to Sleep"

Muddy River Poetry Review: "Prelude to Another Break-up" and "In a Tiny Indian Restaurant"

Rat's Ass Review: "A Straight Bachelor's Last Resort"

Red Eft Review: "Geek Nostalgia"

Red River Review: "Never Date an Egyptologist"

San Pedro River Review: "She Does Not Know Her Wagner"

U.S. 1 Worksheets: "She Just Moved In" and "Earl Grey and a .38"

Verse-Virtual: "Reassure the Phoenix," "Walking at Her Side," "Bowie Knives and a Dropped Eucharist," and "The First of April"

Contents

Part I

Geek Nostalgia	13
First Date Deceptions	15
Never Date an Egyptologist	16
So Much More than an Oil Change	17
Prelude to Another Break-up	19
The Phone Call	20
My Earliest Consolation	21
There Might be a Dragon in Belvedere Castle	23

Part II

Reassure the Phoenix	27
In a Tiny Indian Restaurant	28
A Restless Night and a New Relationship	29
Bad Dream in Mid-REM	30
A Straight Bachelor's Last Resort	31
Ready for the Tsunami	32
She Just Moved In	33
Bonding with the Dog	35
A Seductive Can of Liquid Cheese	36
A Nice Enough Meal	37
Henry	38
Earl Grey and a .38	39
New Ring for an Old Diamond	40
Asking Dad for Her Hand in Marriage	41
Sipping Wine through a Straw	42
Laundry is Easy	43
Walking at Her Side	44
Bowie Knives and a Dropped Eucharist	46
The First of April	48
No Urge to Grieve	49

Part III

Memorial for an Old Friend	53
A Dry Sandwich Made with Love	54
The Day after Registration	55
A Vice-dean Dates Again	56
A Safe Space	57
The Gift that Keeps Giving	58
Cleaning Out My Mother's Closet	60
The Waitress Rolls Her Eyes and Walks Away	62
Blame the Wine	63
Hard to Sleep	65
Fate Meets a College Advisor	66
The Last Bowl of Chili	68
She Does Not Know Her Wagner	69

Part I

Geek Nostalgia

Tired of browsing
an endless succession
of online dating profiles,
I click to another site
start to watch video clips:
toy commercials from the late 1970's,
Star Wars and *Battlestar Galactica*.

I was once that boy
with the X-Wing Fighter
desperate for adventure
imagination growing like a universe.
Those worlds were my homes
and I would fight for them heroically
protecting the innocent
with a handful of friends
earning the love of a beautiful woman.
It would be a life full of purpose
that might end in battle
but it would end
to the sound of a string symphony
the great evil newly vanquished
and they would remember me forever,
worlds of millions
grateful for my sacrifice.

My computer pings.
I switch back to the dating site.
Someone left me a message.

Her name is Lou-Anne
she has five kids
tells me I look like her dead father
wants to meet up for a beer.
The title of her profile reads:
Just Back from Rehab.

First Date Deceptions

She walks into the bookstore
and I see her before she sees me
watch her cautious stride,
the way she looks around.

Her online pictures were deceptive:
an angular pose hid the width of her hips
bright lighting
a turn of the head
masked the pattering of acne scars
the hook of her nose.

Disappointment
like the scratch of a hemp noose
gives way to a tightening.
The trap door opens under my feet
as I reveal myself:
a hidden child who can no longer
evade his kidnapper.

I ask her name knowingly
press gently for a hug.
Her smile reveals a double incisor.
My nose hairs struggle to filter
the baby powder cloud
rising from her skin.

My sister will call me in 57 minutes,
tell me of an emergency
that demands my attention
and I am almost certain
we'll be taking Uncle Clark off life support
before the evening is over.

Never Date an Egyptologist

This is it:
the grand prize for a third date.
Slowly, I enter
relishing the warmth
as it permeates.
My weight settles:
a sinking ship
completing its watery descent.

Face to face
she is expressionless
deep in thought.
I ask if she is ok.
She tells me ancient Egyptian women
inserted crocodile dung
into their vaginal canals
in order to prevent pregnancy

and somewhere between the words
dung and *pregnancy*
I melt like an ice cube
kissed by a blowtorch.

So Much More than an Oil Change

I walk into a car dealership
trying not to look at anyone directly.
Salesmen hiss and lunge
as I make my way to the service department.

A young woman stands by a computer
motions me over with a wink.
Her name is Jacqueline.
She asks where I have been all of her life.

I tell her I need an oil change
for a 2002 Honda Civic.
She closes her eyes and sighs
holds the sides of her desk
as she leans over
revealing her cleavage
says she'll give me anything I want.

The keyboard clatters restlessly.
Her eyes glow blue
from the reflection of the screen.
An oil change is $99.99
($89.99 if I have a coupon).
A recommended 13-point check
that includes a windshield wiper inspection
will bring the total to $299.99, plus tax.

An oil change for my car
should only be about $30.00.
My look of disbelief
prompts her to ask if I am married.
I reply I have been single for years.
Her smile turns my indignation
into a cuddly teddy bear.

A trembling debit card
floats toward her breasts.
Touching my fingers,
she takes the card
mouths a silent thank you,
her tongue moving slowly
over the bottom of her front teeth.

Prelude to Another Break-up

Raven-haired and pale,
she sits at the edge of the bed
cries almost every night I visit
for reasons I do not understand
reasons she will not reveal.
Years ago, she was another woman,
blonde and olive-skinned
and another before this,
brunette and sallow.

Emotion is a war veteran
pitted by inoperable shrapnel
and memory is a fall
down a flight of stairs.
All of those jagged pieces
rattle in their flesh cocoons
bringing back ancient pain,
shouts and screams
tearing through a pool of tinnitus.

Perhaps the Y chromosome,
this ancient, two-pronged arrowhead
keeps me from understanding.
It needs a precise target to be effective
and I don't have the strength
to ask her why again.

Lying on her side,
her sobs become sporadic.
When she falls asleep
I'll leave for home
and try to decide
whether it would be better
to not come back again.

The Phone Call

We broke up two days ago.
I liked her very much
but knew there was no bridge
across the gorge.
The pain would only get worse later.
She didn't take it well
said she would be waiting
in case I changed my mind.

Trying to delete her from my phone
I somehow dialed her number.
An anxious hello followed the first ring
and I became a burglar
caught trying to rob a store
on discount day
for law enforcement officers.
There was nowhere to run.

Clenching my feet,
my toenails bent backwards.
The feeling jolted me to say hello
and apologize for calling
confess I had pushed the wrong button.
Elation disintegrated in the silence.
There was an awkward acknowledgement
two lingering goodbyes:
one from guilt
one from hurt
and I don't know
if she cried after we hung up
but I slept all that night
with a knitting needle
sinking progressively deeper
into my cerebellum.

My Earliest Consolation

Mom, I know my visit is unexpected
but I need your hands
arthritic from worries long past
to steady me once more.

She's been gone for almost a month
but I can still smell her in the sheets.
Her memory lingers
in the paint on the walls.

I'd love to have some homemade soup
but it will be hard to eat.
I feel as if I've been punched in the throat.

The cutting board grunts
while you chat about the weather
and the idiots next door.
Steam warms my face.
Basil leaves hide my eyes.

When you tell me
she was no good,
that you always knew
but could never say,
part of me hopes
you'll tug my head up
call me a damn fool

and run your carving knife
across my throat
so creamy tomato
can finally soothe my suffering.

Instead, you put a sandwich by the soup
turkey and Swiss
cut diagonally, without the crust,
just the way I've always liked it.

There Might be a Dragon in Belvedere Castle

Our first date fell on Halloween,
Celtic Samhain
when the spirits of the dead
can walk among the living.

I am one of these ghosts
walking the footpaths of Central Park
trying to find Belvedere Castle.

We met online.
Her name is Emily:
a model with a love
for writing and photography
lives with her dog on the Upper West Side.
I wrote to a teacher as well
but she never responded
though we do very similar jobs,
kindergarten and college advising.

I'm not sure why I suggested this place,
a two-hour train ride
from central New Jersey
but she lives in New York
and dinner or coffee
can get a bit boring
when one has been dating for twenty-five years.

Sitting on a rock
surrounded by trees
the little urban fortress comes into view.
A string quartet plays Bach somewhere nearby.

Could this be where the fairy tale begins
and the jester finds his lady
or will she be a dragon
in Louis Vuitton boots
clawing me to death
to the second Brandenburg Concerto?

Part II

Reassure the Phoenix

I imagine you in a blizzard
trying to keep afloat
within an ocean of cancer medication
watching me on the shoreline
waiting for me to find shelter
before you stop swimming.

You want me to find someone
as most mothers do
so I won't be alone
holding my hand
as we walk through a maze
of half-buried mirror shards
pulling me onwards
more vehemently now than ever before
stabbing me gently
with a blunt-tipped bayonet
as you tell me to brush
the lint from my tuxedo jacket.

After decades of searching
there are more than a few
holes in the fabric
and cut marks on my face.
Even you bleed
though you try to hide it.

Desperation never suited you.
I would rather have you with me
enjoying the time that remains
than watch new love rise
like a phoenix from your ashes.

In a Tiny Indian Restaurant

Another dinner date
the 51st or 89th this year
the second one for Emily and me
at a tiny Indian restaurant
on Lexington Avenue.

I waited nearly a week
took two trains
walked nearly forty blocks
to see those lips again
and green eyes
like rain-soaked forests
sparkling in an ocean
of cars and dirty concrete.

It could be true chemistry
or desire held back by caution
a rusted cage full of starving dogs
who bang their bleeding heads
against the bars
iron oxide tongues dripping.

This tablecloth and I have much in common
stained and torn in places not so obvious.
The room's romantic lighting
works to my advantage.

She steps on my foot.
Our knees bang together
making the ice rattle in our water glasses.
We laugh and I forget
how hard it is to find
someone I really want.

A Restless Night and a New Relationship

It is my first sleepover with Emily.
Her Saint Bernard lies at the foot of the bed.
She kisses me goodnight
just before I turn out the light.

In the darkness, I start to hear him:
jingle
yawn
whine
burp
jingle
yelp
chomp
smack
whine
the smell of putrid gas hits my nose
jingle
yelp
a mid-dream bark
awakens me even more.

The clock crawls past midnight
sprints to 2:00 a.m.
and through it all
she
still
sleeps
unperturbed.

Bad Dream in Mid-REM

I lie on the asphalt
like a dead deer
victim of a hit and run.
It may have been an ice cream truck.
I heard the glockenspiel version
of *Born to be Wild*
before everything went dark.

People come out of stores and cars
passersby stop and walk over:
a kaleidoscope of bobbing heads
sucks up my oxygen
replaces it with latte-spiked
carbon dioxide.

Someone asks me if I am ok
and texts someone else
before I can answer.
Someone in the back of the crowd
gives me a Hitler salute
with his smartphone.
A camera flash obscures
my already blurry vision.

A lawyer puts his business card
into my shirt pocket
tells me to call him
while two EMT's strap me to a gurney.
One of them takes a selfie
of all three of us
our cheeks pressed together
like we were old friends.
It's his first day on the job
and he wanted to remember the moment.

A Straight Bachelor's Last Resort

Lying in a dentist's chair
a middle-aged hygienist grunts
as she scrapes the tartar from my teeth,
feet curl from sensitive gums.

She tells me her husband
no longer finds her attractive.
With the taste of blood in my mouth
I emit a pitying hum.

Looking deeply into my eyes
she says she knows how to use
every centimeter of the human tongue
and is willing to show me if I want.

Her breast pushes up against my shoulder.
I could tell her I am not interested
but rejection might turn
her dental pick into a dagger.
I could tell her I am dating someone
but it doesn't seem like she would care.

Gently pushing her hand away
I tell her I am gay
that Bill and I are very happy together.
There might even be
a church in Vermont
with our names on it.

Her face crinkles in disappointment
resembles a Renaissance fresco.
She mumbles her congratulations
tosses a little tube of toothpaste on my lap
and tells me to floss more often.

Ready for the Tsunami

That word,
the one stronger than like
leaves a film on my skin
makes my nerves screech
like inserting the tip of a knife
into a hole made
by a freshly pulled tooth.

Even when I feel it
I'd rather show it than say it.
This never quite worked in a relationship.

We've been dating for over six months
and it was easy to ask her
if we could be exclusive
as I never wanted a competitor.
I am by nature, territorial.
That word is different,
a rain-slicked racetrack,
infantry combat
where survival earns rank:
co-habitation
engagement
marriage
children (perish the thought)
checking one another
for discolored moles
without the slightest embarrassment.

I ran from it in my 20's
power walked to safety at 35
strolled away casually at 40.
At 44, I am a man with a limp
who hears the tsunami roar
smiles and lights a cigarette.

She Just Moved In

I lie on the floor
frayed and worn out
held together with safety pins
like the tweed jacket
of a New York City Hipster.

The contents of Emily's apartment
have turned my condo
into the excavated treasure chambers
of an ancient people
with very poor taste in furniture.
Searching for her second-favorite teddy bear,
she buried me under her bedding
without knowing I was there.

But it is paradise under this pile,
the heart of a mountain
of duvets and comforters
blankets and quilts
throw pillows, bed pillows
cushions and Afghans:
a little hard to breathe
heavy on my chest
but I like the darkness
and the feeling of no longer existing.

She calls my name
walks past me three times.
Her ancient Saint Bernard follows behind
tries to sniff me out
but the rose-scented fabric softener
she uses on her sheets

makes me just another piece
of Egyptian cotton
with a 300-thread count
waiting for the next inundation
of mascara stains and dog drool.

Bonding with the Dog

Bloated ticks fly
from my girlfriend's dog, Sampson
as he shakes off the rain
in the middle of my living room.
Muddy specks coat the walls
and the recently-dusted
cherry wood coffee table.

He looks up at me and whines
and I wish he was a cat
or better yet
a ceramic umbrella holder
that sits silently in the foyer.

I ask him if he'd like
to live somewhere else far away.
He lifts his paw but loses his balance
crushes a tick as he lands,
leaves a thumbnail-sized blotch
of coagulated red
on my brand new off-white carpet.

A Seductive Can of Liquid Cheese

Grocery shopping used to be so easy
twenty minutes in and out:
a sailor in a whorehouse
a few soup cans and frozen dinners
a twelve-pack of iced tea
and I'd be set for the week.

There weren't many customers at 10 p.m.
nurses and security guards
just getting off duty
weekday drunks
and aimless degenerates
who spent half an hour trying to decide
between name brand
and generic baking soda.

Now, I wander through crowded aisles
on Saturday morning
following my intended.
She tells me we need to find organic kumquats
as she looks for foods I never knew existed:
watercress and hearts of palm
taro crackers and boysenberry jam.

I push the overloaded cart
past the potato chip section
wistfully brush my fingertips
over a can of liquid cheese.

A Nice Enough Meal

Emily puts a plate in front of me.
Steam rises from a piece of grilled chicken
and a handful of miniature carrots and potatoes.
Her stare burns a hole in my lower lip
as I take the first bite:
How is it?
Too dry?
Did I use enough pepper?
Did it cook through enough?
Are the potatoes too hard?
Should I have made rolls?

I tell her the meal is very good.
Everything is just fine
but her eyes well with tears.
I'm doing the best I can!
I don't cook very often!

Running into the bedroom,
she slams the door behind her.
I sigh and smile weakly
thinking about my mother
who would unceremoniously drop
a slab of meatloaf on my plate.
When I looked up at her
disappointed at her dinner choice
she'd glare at me and say:
If you don't like it,
Gino's Pizza is right down the road.
Take your father with you.

Henry

He sits in the place
where I used to display
my Darth Vader Tie Fighter:
a pink, fluffy, overstuffed hippo
my girlfriend bought
when she lived in New York City.

His round black eyes follow me
when I walk around the bedroom,
when I get dressed for work.
They peer at me during sex.
I can hear him speak to me telepathically:
If I had the right anatomy, she'd be mine
and you'd be dating a fat girl from Metuchen.

She kisses him good night
cradles him in bed.
Sometimes I wake
to find him sitting on my chest
or perched on my groin
looking up at me with his red-stitched smile:
If you get into a fatal car accident today
don't worry,
I'll be here to comfort
my beloved Emily.

Earl Grey and a .38

Emily puts a cup of tea in front of me
loads five bullets
into a six-shot revolver
spins the cylinder
lays the gun next to the teacup.

Chewing a mouthful of Advil,
wincing from cramps
she asks what I meant
when I wished the cashier at Walgreen's
a good day,
wonders if I often flirt
with women half my age.
Before I can respond,
she points to the gun.
I pick it up and put it to my temple.

She asks if I love her.
My response is a yes,
that if I was Odysseus
she would be my Scylla and Charybdis
especially at times like this.

I pull the trigger and hear a click.
She looks at me suspiciously
unfamiliar with Greek mythology
but eventually nods her approval,
and asks me to empty the dishwasher
before I go to bed.

New Ring for an Old Diamond

Mom gave me her engagement ring:
a replacement dad bought
for the one stolen on their honeymoon,
gave me the name of a jeweler
who would replace the setting
without robbing me blind.

I felt awkward accepting it,
but her voice had that
son-obey-your-mother tone
with a firmness undiminished
by months of chemo and radiation.

The diamond is a shatterproof tear,
a representation
of all the worry I caused her:
a strange and awkward boy
who liked books more than people
growing with the years
into a sullen bachelor
who liked books more than people.
A heavy stone fell from her shoulders
when I told her I had found *the one*.

Soon, this ring will have a new setting
white gold for new love
crowned with an old love
an amalgam
unbreakable and enduring,
an ever-present
reminder of sacrifice.

Asking Dad for Her Hand in Marriage

Her father is in his living room
sitting on a recliner
watching a football game.
I hold out my hand and he nods
tells me to sit down.

Black-rimmed glasses glow
from the light of the TV.
A chili cheese nacho
and imported beer belly
rise and fall
like a burial mound
trying to disgorge its dead.

He says he loves his daughter
and he's a traditional man.
Am I good enough for her?
Do I come from a decent family?
Can I advance in my career?

I tell him I am better
than her last husband:
a coke-snorting poker addict,
the one he previously approved.
My parents have been married
for over forty years
longer than all of his marriages combined.
I never cheated on a woman
never got caught embezzling company funds
never claimed to be traditional
when I was not.
I also sincerely detest football.
He asks me to leave.
I say the wedding is next June.

Sipping Wine through a Straw

I am sitting across from my girlfriend
in a restored railway car
from the 1920's
traveling through the Bucks County countryside
trying to work a marriage proposal
into our conversation.

When she looks around
to admire the wood paneling,
I take out the ring
clear my throat and say:
Emily, can we be that 50%
that don't wind up divorced?
Better yet
can we be that 20%
that aren't miserable
staying together out of habit
or from fear of starting over
when we are even less desirable?

She says yes
and a waiter brings us
two plastic cups of wine,
lidded with straws coming out of the tops.
Reading our faces
he tells us glassware is too fragile
for the bumps and lurches of the train ride.

Drinking wine like an eight-year-old
was the only part of the occasion
that disappointed me.

Laundry is Easy

I do laundry for my parents
when mom is in the hospital
because dad never learned
and he never wears
the same pair of sweatpants twice.

There is not much else to do.
I cannot shrink the tumor
nestled like a Japanese beetle
on her pancreas.
I cannot find the words
to reassure my father
everything will turn out right
and mom will be
that 5 or 7% they say
make it to five years.

Love and sadness are hard to express
vulnerability is uncomfortable
but laundry is easy.
A machine does most of the work
and in only a couple of hours
what was once dirty
comes out clean and sweet-smelling
ready to be folded and put away
like a delusional feeling of accomplishment.

Walking at Her Side

I can't remember the last time
we walked alone
side by side.
I was probably a child
sometime in the 70's
or very early 80's,
vague memories
when we both had different clothes
and different hair.

The floors of the hospital corridors gleam
contrast with the walls,
scuffed black and chipped
intermittently.
I have a hard time moving at her pace.
At well over six feet,
smaller strides make me clumsy.

We are mostly silent.
She seems to be in another place
and I look around
trying to distract myself
watch the nurses
working at their stations
see the other patients
lying in their beds,
sleeping or watching TV.

The beeping of her monitor
makes my next exclamation
seem like a detonation
when I tell her I am now
engaged to be married.

My mother nods
tells me it's good
lets out a sigh
that could be exhaustion
or her way of saying
it's about fucking time.

Bowie Knives and a Dropped Eucharist

The hospital chaplain
came to visit my mother,
asked her if she wanted Communion.

Head bowed,
a golden bowl of wafers in her hand
the chaplain asked for the intercession
of Jesus, Mary, and St. Michael
and I could not help but smirk
being 99% atheist
reserving only that 1%
for the possibility of a disinterested
prime mover.

When she placed the Host
on my mother's dry tongue,
I imagined her pancreas
as a saloon in the Old West
where a malignant tumor
throws a drink of whiskey
in the face of her diabetes.
They draw Bowie Knives
and slash one another red.

During the prayer
one wafer fell from the bowl.
I was the only one who noticed
but kept silent
even after the service was over.

Stay on the floor,
body of Christ.
Bless the feet of the nurse

who runs from room to room.
Bless the mop of the janitor
that has to clean
my mother's sick.

The First of April

We brought mom home from the hospital
put a bed in the living room
so she could be cared for more easily.

Her last day had the atmosphere
of a mid-nineteenth century novel.
It rained hard that night
and into the morning.
The streetlight made a lazy hail
look like snow.

I was a bridge between Emily
and my dying mother,
holding their hands
imagining a torch pass
from one to the other
translating her unconscious moaning:
Look out for your father.
Be a good husband.
Try not to be an asshole at work.

I slept on the couch
but woke up periodically
to see if her chest
was still rising and falling.
I saw her breathing even after she stopped.

The storm ended after she died.
I took out the garbage
needing an excuse
to get out of the house
saw the gray glow of early dawn
heard the faint sound of birds.

No Urge to Grieve

I did not cry
when my mother died.
I don't know why.
Maybe tears are finite
and I used them all on broken toys
or my failed relationships
before realizing
a failed relationship
was usually a good thing.

It's possible I'll feel the urge tomorrow
or years from now.
Music might trigger it:
a symphony by Mahler,
a film score depicting
the death of a movie hero
and I'll shatter like a rock
taken out of a river
and thrown into a fire.

Sampson looks up at me
whining to go out
and even though it's cold outside
I welcome the distraction.

Part III

Memorial for an Old Friend

We scattered your ashes today, dear friend
though you died nearly three years ago:
a quiet cove on the mountain lake
where you always dreamed of living.
The cloud you made as you entered the water
was beautiful and transient.
We drank whiskey right after
to celebrate your Irish pride.

As you dissipated in the water,
I thought about my mother
gone now almost two months,
how you both sped up the process
of flesh to dust,
how you both leave men behind
widowed and rudderless.
You were the nails of an old Victorian house
pulled out by a giant magnet.
Age and pressure is what keeps us together now.

I do not believe in heaven or hell
but I will resurrect you in my memory
from time to time
seat you at a table with those already gone.
You will have purple drinking glasses
plates painted with smiling suns.
My mother will have a seat right next to you
but not just yet.
That is still too soon for me to imagine.

A Dry Sandwich Made with Love

My colleagues pass by
holding plastic trays and paper plates.
The smell of microwaved cheese
and two-day old haddock
pour from the kitchen
like a sewer pipe in a sub-tropical city.
I shut my office door
so I can eat without gagging.

Emily now makes my lunch
claiming my years as a bachelor
have fostered very bad habits.
Today is unsalted turkey
lettuce and fat free mayonnaise
on whole wheat bread.
For dessert, she packed pomegranate seeds
which, I believe, were used in medieval times
as an aphrodisiac.

She wants me to live well past a hundred
to an age when a burly nurse
with a thick accent
will have to chew my food
and spit it into my mouth
as if I was a senile baby bird.

My molars grind into the dry and bland sandwich
like reluctant executioners.
I wouldn't mind dying at seventy
if I could do so with a colon full of burgers.
My wife might cry at first
but when she reads my insurance policy
it might console her to find out
I am worth far more dead than alive.

The Day after Registration

The phone rings with urgency
but I do not pick it up.
It's the same student
for the fifth time:
finance major
future hedge fund sociopath
who can't accept no for an answer.

The titles of incoming e-mails
warn of fabricated tragedy:
Urgent!
Please Help!!
Need Appointment Now!!!
I delete them without reading.

We sent them several reminders
sent letters to their campus mailbox
text messages to their phones
put the deadline in bold letters
but there is always a group
that eats the yellow snow
even when we warn against it.

A secretary enters my office
while I'm closing down for the day
says a student needs to see me
about adding art history to her schedule
won't leave until she does.
I nod and exit through the back door
hoping the student
ate and used the bathroom
before she left her house
as I won't be back for another three days.

A Vice-dean Dates Again

He climbs out of his two-seater sports car
fifty-five and newly divorced
ready to date
make the ex-wife rage with jealousy.

Executive vice-dean of a for-profit college
PhD in academic administration
and seduction.
He's been practicing flirtation
with freshmen girls
learning what a young woman likes to hear
how to be intriguing and mysterious.

Hair plugs convincingly blend
into his upper scalp
anti-gas pills
and a condom from 2004
sit in his left breast pocket.
It's time for some action.

A thick-necked bouncer
opens the door to the dance club.
He stumbles on the threshold
regains his balance
smoothes the sleeves
of his dark blue blazer
and promises himself
that will be the last mistake
he makes tonight.

A Safe Space

A frustrated freshman sits in my office
tells me she's been a student
at my crappy university for over a month
and still cannot find a safe space.
Her former high school had three of them.
She wants to know their location.

Misunderstanding her question,
I tell her my office is not that safe:
the sheet rock walls are very thin
the locks are poorly made.
It would not take much
for a shooter to break down the door.
We could hide under the desk
but a high caliber projectile
can go right through the formica.
Escape through a window is not possible.
We are on the twelfth floor.
They also cut the security budget
to give the football coach a 20% raise.

The student huffs
leaves without a goodbye
or an apology for wasting my time.
An eavesdropping colleague
pokes her head into the doorway
tells me a safe space is for students to escape
from the pressures and judgments
of the outside world.

We both laugh.

The Gift that Keeps Giving

Emily's ex-husband
shares joint custody with the dog.
Every first weekend of the month
he comes to pick him up.

I am kneeling in the flower garden
when a fire red sports car
pulls into a nearby parking space.
The engine revs loudly.

The car door opens.
I can smell his cologne
from fifty-feet away.
His clothing gives off the aura
of a gentrified Mid-towner
who spends his work week
robbing the elderly of their life savings:
white silk shirt opened at the collar
distressed brown leather jacket
overpriced sunglasses
made by Chinese slave labor.

Our eyes meet.
I nod.
He smirks
and I wonder
if the azalea I am planting
could fit into one of his orifices.

My fiancée brings out Sampson.
Her ex-husband touches her chin
as she frowns,
wordlessly hands over the leash.

His alligator boots scrape
the concrete walkway
as he gives us a smug goodbye.
I reply the dog just had his dinner
neglecting to mention it was hot dogs.
Sampson loves hot dogs
although they tend to give him
severe and frequent flatulence.

Cleaning Out My Mother's Closet

I enter the bedroom
open my mother's closet door
spread a plastic garbage bag
on the floor at my feet.

My father is sitting in the next room
looking at her pictures
like a child trying to pretend
his parents aren't arguing.

Skirts and blouses
jeans and sweaters
crowd the plastic hangers.
I pull them off
one at a time
drop them in the bag.
Short bursts of radio static
grow fainter as it fills.

She was her father's daughter.
Grandpop loved clothes, too:
a child of the Depression
loath to throw anything away.
Twenty-five years ago
I cleaned out his closets.
My outward lack of sentimentality
makes me ideal for tasks like these.

Clearing out the top shelf
I find a square box
wrapped in red paper
with a half-crushed green bow on top.

The card is addressed to me,
a Christmas gift she probably forgot
to give me last year.

I put it back on the shelf,
hide it in a corner.
It will likely be much easier
to open next year.

The Waitress Rolls Her Eyes and Walks Away

Our hostess takes us to a table,
the last one in the diner.
Next to us,
a father and mother gaze at their smartphones
while a toddler shrieks between them.
Its face is smeared
congealed blue.
Plate shards and corn kernels
surround the legs of its high chair.

Emily and I look at each other.
In our minds, we pick the parent
we would use as a shield
if a maniac came in shooting.

I'm glad she dislikes children
and inconsiderate parents
almost as much as I do
though I sometimes worry
she'll change her mind.
I'll be trying to chase a child
with my future artificial hip
praying for an artery to burst
and deliver me from middle-age fatherhood.

A pregnant waitress takes our order.
Over the wailing of the toddler,
I choose the lamb.
My fiancée orders the veal
adds we both love the taste of baby meat.

Blame the Wine

I run over a squirrel
on the way home from dinner.
It was unintentional
but I didn't feel that bad.

Emily begins to cry
as I look in the rear-view mirror.
She asks if it might only be hurt.
I watch its death convulsions
purse my lips and shake my head.

She tells me I had too much wine
wants to go back
so she can see for herself
suggests we take it to a veterinarian.

I turn the car around
as she comments
on my illegal k-turn
my lack of lightning reflexes.
The roar of the engine
temporarily drowns
the sound of her whining.

Slowing down to the speed
of a gangland drive-by,
we see a lump of gray fur
surrounded by a red pool.
A crow jumps from a low branch,
starts to nibble at the lifeless animal.

She looks at me and wipes her eyes
consoles herself with the thought
the birds will have something to eat.
I nod and drive away,
grateful for my inability to see
the lighter side of things.

Hard to Sleep

We never hold each other
while we sleep
because the beating of my heart
disturbs her.
She compares it
to a psychotic gremlin
beating a drum
again and again.

No woman has ever said this
to me before.
Most of them have liked my heartbeat
at least at first.
Then, they want it to stop.
Sometimes, by natural means.
Sometimes, impaled
by a fireplace poker
or a shard of steering wheel.

I have often thought
the same about them.

Fate Meets a College Advisor

Resting from an afternoon hike
I watch the late August sun descend
behind the Sourland Mountains.

Something brushes my shoulder
and a trickle of liquid nitrogen
slides down my spine
like a fireman's pole.

An apparition appears:
a dark gray cloak made of ashes.
My hiking pole turns into a snake
that binds my hands together.

It hovers several feet off the ground.
Terrified, I stammer out:
Are you death?
Has my time finally come?

It laughs like crackling ice:
No. I am the coming school year
and I bring even more students than before
impatient and entitled
unappreciative and rude
for the same money you made last year.

A black hole opens
in the center of its hood
and 1200 buzzing locusts,
one for every student I will have
swarm directly at my face.
I want to scream
but I can't open my mouth.

Awakening with a jolt
damp and frightened
I am now in my bed.
It was a nightmare
at least the part about the apparition.
Half-asleep, Emily rolls over
tells me to stop moaning
reminds me it's garbage day today.

The Last Bowl of Chili

It looks like the heart
of a prehistoric creature,
red and covered with frost.
It takes me a moment
but I remember what it is:
a container of leftover chili
my mother made the month before she died.

I put it in the microwave
watch it slowly revolve.
The smells release as it thaws:
beef and tomato sauce
a sharp sting of onion and green pepper
a dash of cayenne.
This was the smell of Labor Day and 4th of July
my childhood and teens
stretching out in a trail of warm grease
to a middle-aged man
blowing steam from a bowl.

She's been gone for almost four months
but the taste is undiminished.
I don't know if I'll get sick later on
but I really don't care.

This is the last food my mother made
that I will ever eat.
Even if I knew the recipe
it would never be the same
and I'm glad my father is taking a nap
glad Emily is out of town for work.
No one will witness
my granite skin crumble
as I struggle to swallow the last mouthful.

She Does Not Know Her Wagner

She loves the *Wedding March*
first practiced it when she was seven
did it for real
but with the wrong man
at twenty-five.
Now, at thirty-eight
she wants to do it again with me.

I mention absent-mindedly
it's from an opera by Wagner.
A brave knight appears
on a boat drawn by a swan,
marries a beautiful lady.

Emily smiles
until I tell her
the lady betrays the knight.
He then leaves her and she dies of grief.

Luckily, decades of bachelorhood
have acclimated me
to dead silence and cold dinner.

About the Author

John David Muth is a resident of central New Jersey. He has been an academic advisor at Rutgers University for eighteen years. In his spare time, he enjoys hiking, road trips, and volunteering for environmental causes. His poetry satirizes the absurdities often found in romantic relationships, societal values, and cultural practices. He is a member of the U.S. 1 Poet's Cooperative. His work has appeared in such journals as *Anti-Heroin Chic, Verse-Virtual, San Pedro River Review,* and *U.S. 1 Worksheets.* He is the author of three collections of poetry: *A Love for Lavender Dragons* (Aldrich Press, 2016)*, Inevitable Carbon* (Aldrich Press, 2017), and *Odysseus in Absaroka* (Aldrich Press, 2018).

www.ingramcontent.com/pod-product-compliance
Lightning Source LLC
LaVergne TN
LVHW091319080426
835510LV00007B/562